DK Watch me grow
Frog

DK

LONDON, NEW YORK, MUNICH,
MELBOURNE and DELHI

Written and edited by Lisa Magloff
Designed by Sonia Whillock,
Mary Sandberg, and Sadie Thomas

Publishing Manager Sue Leonard
Managing Art Editor Clare Shedden
Jacket Design Katy Wall
Picture Researcher Julia Harris Voss
Production Shivani Pandey
DTP Designer Almudena Díaz
Consultant Barbara Taylor

First American Edition, 2003
Published in the United States by
DK Publishing, Inc.
375 Hudson Street
New York, New York 10014

03 04 05 06 07 08 09 10 9 8 7 6 5 4 3 2

Copyright © 2003 Dorling Kindersley Limited

A Cataloging-in-Publication record for this book
is available from the Library of Congess
ISBN 0-7894-9629-1

Colour reproduction by
GRB Editrice S.r.l., Verona, Italy.
Printed and bound by
South China Printing Co, Ltd., China

see our complete product line at
www.dk.com

Hop off with me and watch me GROW...

Contents

I'm a frog

I like to croak. I have slippery skin. I live in water and on land. I have long legs and I can leap very high.

A frog's skin is soft and wet.

Here I am with some of my froggie friends in our pond.

4

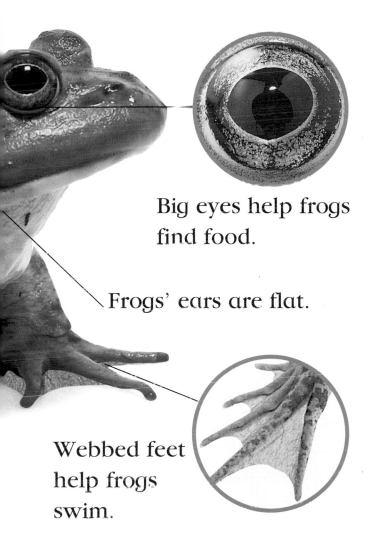

Big eyes help frogs find food.

Frogs' ears are flat.

Webbed feet help frogs swim.

Splish! Splash!
Frogs love water. Look for them in ponds, rivers, or squelchy marshes.

Turn the page and find out how my life began.

Before I was born

Mom laid thousands of eggs in a pond, and then Dad fertilized them. To do this, he had to stay very close to Mom while she laid all her eggs.

A group of eggs is called frog spawn.

Calling all frogs
Croaking is the frog's version of talking. Croaking is how male frogs tell female frogs where they are.

Dad held onto mom while she laid her eggs.

Mom's tummy
is full of eggs.

Spawn facts

🐸 The mother frog can lay
as many as 4000 eggs.

🐸 Frog spawn have food
inside them for the growing
tadpole babies to eat.

Now I'm growing inside my egg

I already have my tail and gills. In a few days, I will be big enough to wriggle out.

Beginning of life
A frog's life begins as a tiny black egg. The jelly around the egg protects it from bumps.

After nine days, a tadpole is almost ready to hatch out.

Jelly facts

🐸 Frog spawn floats to the surface of the water and is warmed by the sun.

🐸 The jelly swells in the water to protect the egg.

🐸 The tadpole hatches out after about 10 days.

After 10 days I start to push through the sticky jelly.

9

I'm ready to hatch out

Once I am out of my egg, I swim up to the surface of the pond, where it's warm and there's plenty of food.

Hundreds of tadpoles hatch at the same time.

It takes all day for a tadpole to work its way out of the egg.

After hatching, tadpoles rest for a few minutes before swimming off.

Great gills
Tadpoles can breathe in the water because they have gills that can take in air that is in the water.

11

After four weeks, my teeth begin to grow

At last I can start eating insects. When a big, tasty worm drifts down from the surface, I share it with my brothers and sisters.

Tadpoles use their tiny teeth to chew their food.

Tadpole facts

 By four weeks, a tadpole's gills are covered in skin, and its lungs begin to grow.

 Most tadpoles are eaten before they can grow up.

Danger lurks

Other creatures in the pond are also looking for food. Tadpoles have to move fast to get away from a hungry trout.

These tadpoles are too quick for me!

Now I'm part tadpole and part frog

When I am six weeks old, my arms and legs start to grow. My new legs help me swim. I am part tadpole and part frog. I have become a froglet.

Look, no arms!
A froglet's back legs are the first to grow, and then its front legs grow. The froglet's body and head also start to grow much bigger.

The tail gets shorter as the legs begin to paddle.

This bug will make a great snack.

Froglets eat bugs like this crunchy water boatman.

Froglet facts

🐸 It takes about 14 weeks for a froglet to turn into a frog.

🐸 The froglet now has lungs and breathes by quickly swimming to the surface to gulp some air.

Now I'm ready to leave the water

After three months, I breathe through my lungs and even my skin. Now I am ready to start living on land.

Going, going, gone!
When I am 13 weeks old,
my tail is almost gone.
Just a tiny bit is left.

I'm so small, I can sit on your fingertip.

After three years I'll be as BIG as your fist.

Growing facts

· · · · · · · · · · · · · · ·

🐸 An adult frog is 10 times bigger than when it first came out of the water.

🐸 Summer is the best time to spot new adult frogs.

I leap from land to water

I need to keep my skin wet to stay
healthy, so after eating on land,
I leap back into the water for a swim.

Ready... steady... GO!

Leaping facts

- If you could hop like a frog, you would be able to cross a football field in just four jumps.

- Frogs don't just hop for fun, they also hop to catch food and to escape from animals that want to eat them.

Long reach
A frog's tongue is attached to the front of its mouth, not the back, so it can reach farther for yummy bugs.

Look out, here I come...splash!

The circle of life goes around and around

Now you know how I turned into a slippery frog.

Croak, croak. See you next spring.

My friends from around the world

The tiny tree frog is as big as your fingernail.

The bright green Tinker Reed Frog is one of the loudest frogs.

The White's Tree Frog from Australia can live for more than 21 years.

This Poison Dart Frog is brightly colored to warn enemies to stay away.

The Bumpy Horned Frog is

My frog friends all around the world come in different colors and shapes to help them survive in the place where they live.

The Bullfrog has a huge appetite.

This Tomato frog looks like his name—red and round!

also called "a mouth with legs."

FuN frog facts
. . . .

🐸 The world's largest frog is the Goliath Frog of West Africa. It grows to 1 foot (300mm) long.

🐸 Some frogs can kill a person with their poison.

🐸 In 1977, a South African Sharp-Nosed Frog set a record for the froggie triple jump— 33 feet 5 inches (10 meters).

Glossary

Webbing
Thin skin that connects the frog's toes and helps it swim.

Gills
A part of the tadpole's body that helps it breathe.

Frog spawn
What frogs' eggs are called when they are all together.

Tadpole
Newly hatched frog tadpoles have tails and live in the water.

Hatch
When a baby frog hatches, it comes out of its egg.

Froglet
In between a tadpole and a frog. Arms and legs are growing.

Acknowledgments
The publisher would like to thank the following for their kind permission to reproduce their photographs:
(Key: a=above; c=centre; b=below; l=left; r=right; t=top)
1: Getty images/David Aubrey c; 2-3: ImageState Pictor Ltd/Paul Wenham-Clarke; 4-5: Getty Images; 5: Getty Images tr; 6: Stuart R. Harrop bl; 7: FLPA - Images of Nature/Derek Middleton c; 8: N.H.P.A./Roger Tidman l; 9: N.H.P.A./Stephen Dalton c; 10-11: ImageState Pictor Ltd; 11: Stuart R. Harrop/Prof. br; 12: N.H.P.A./Stephen Dalton c; 13: Getty Images br; 14-15: N.H.P.A./G. I. Bernard; 16-17: Getty Images; 17: ImageState Pictor Ltd/Paul Wenham-Clarke r; 18-19: ImageState Pictor Ltd/Paul Wenham-Clarke; 19: N.H.P.A./Stephen Dalton cr; 20: N.H.P.A./Laurie Campbell c; Stephen Dalton tcl; 23: Jerry Young tr; 24: N.H.P.A./Roger Tidman cl.

Jacket Front: Jerry Young bc.

All other images © Dorling Kindersley
For further information see: www.dkimages.com